D1472659

The Library of Explorers and Exploration

JACQUES CARTIER

Navigating the St. Lawrence River

Meg Greene

the rosen publishing group's
rosen
central

For Bill, Chip, and Phillip

Published in 2004 by The Rosen Publishing Group, Inc.
29 East 21st Street, New York, NY 10010

First Edition

Library of Congress Cataloging-in-Publication Data

Greene, Meg.
Jacques Cartier: navigating the St. Lawrence River / Meg Greene. — 1st ed.
    p. cm. — (The library of explorers and exploration)
Summary: Describes the life and travels of Jacques Cartier, the sixteenth-
century French navigator who made three voyages to what is today
known as Canada, in search of a northwest passage to China.
ISBN 0-8239-3624-4 (library binding)
1. Cartier, Jacques, 1491–1557—Juvenile literature. 2. Explorers—
America—Biography—Juvenile literature. 3. Explorers—France—
Biography—Juvenile literature. 4. Canada—Discovery and
exploration—Juvenile literature. 5. Saint Lawrence River—Discovery
and exploration—Juvenile literature. 6. Canada—History—To 1763
(New France)—Juvenile literature. [1. Cartier, Jacques, 1491–1557.
2. Explorers. 3. Canada—Discovery and exploration. 4. Canada—
History—To 1763 (New France)]
I. Title. II. Series.
E133.C3 M27 2003
971.01'13'092—dc21
                                                        2002000483

Manufactured in the United States of America

CONTENTS

Jacques Cartier was a French sailor and explorer who claimed the St. Lawrence River region for France. This illustration shows him with a globe and, the map in the background displays the seas next to the New World. Cartier explored the Gulf of St. Lawrence seeking riches and a route to Asia. He died still believing that the St. Lawrence led to the fabled kingdom of Saguenay.

INTRODUCTION

BREAKING THE BOUNDS OF EUROPE

This see is called the Great Occyan
So great it is that never man
Coude tell it sith the worlde begane
Tyll now, within this twenty. Yeare
Westwarde be founde new landes
—From the English play by John Rastell, *Interlude of the Nature of the Four Elements*, c. 1518

For almost a thousand years, European civilization had been confined to a compact peninsula attached to the Asian continent. European attempts to expand beyond the frontiers of Europe—the Crusades, a series of religious wars fought during the eleventh and twelfth centuries—had failed. As a consequence, until the end of the fifteenth century, the world that Europeans knew was a rather narrow place.

By the end of the fifteenth century, however, new advancements had been made in navigational technology, such as the invention of the compass. The gradual rise of the nation-state—centralized kingdoms, such as those found in Portugal, Spain, France, and England—facilitated

5

the creation of new wealth. Most important, the vision of a few powerful men and women helped Europe embark on a series of remarkable journeys that eventually carried them to the four corners of the earth.

These overseas adventures were fueled by the desire to gain a foothold in the East—a seemingly exotic land to the Europeans that they believed contained great wealth in silks, spices, gold, and other valuable commodities. During the Middle Ages, widespread stories characterized the East as overflowing with treasure. European adventurers, merchants, bankers, and rulers entertained high hopes of finding precious metals and jewels, expanding trade and markets, and acquiring spices in Asia. Since the thirteenth century, Europeans had been captivated by merchants such as Marco Polo, whose journeys to the Far East (from 1271 until 1295) were filled with tales of wondrous sights and fabulous riches.

The quest for spices was very important. Spices such as pepper entered Europe via Arab and Venetian merchants. But spices were outrageously expensive. Rising prices and limited supply did nothing to diminish the demand. European merchants sought to break the Arab and Venetian monopoly on the spice trade, which elevated their costs and diminished their profits, by going directly to the source themselves. That meant they would have to find some means of getting to India and China to gain access to pepper

Nutmeg and mace were some of the most prized spices during Cartier's time. Both are derived from the same plant: Nutmeg is the kernel, not the nut, of an apricot-like fruit. Mace is the arillus, a thin leathery tissue between the stone and the pulp. Other sought-after spices included black pepper, cloves, and cinammon.

and the other spices they wanted. The incentive for economic and territorial expansion gave rise to the desire to explore the world. Another important motive for the expansion of Europe was religious zeal. Military and religious rivalry between the Christian and Muslim worlds had been a constant of European politics throughout the Middle Ages. At one time or another between the eighth and sixteenth centuries, Muslims ruled not only the whole of North Africa, but many European territories as well: Spain, Portugal, Sicily, the Balkans, and parts of Central Europe.

To Europeans, the inhabitants, flora, and fauna of Canada were very exotic. This hand-colored lithograph illustrates the process involved in killing a seal or walrus in order to re-sell the pelts in stores.

But travel to Asia meant a long, expensive, and hazardous journey. Some explorers, such as Christopher Columbus, Ferdinand Magellan, and Vasco Nuñez de Balboa, thought that a quicker way to the East lay in sailing the oceans to the west. Sooner or later, these mariners reasoned, European ships sailing west would surely reach Asia. There was no question that such a journey would be dangerous; it was also clear that the rewards would be unimaginably great for the kingdom that first found the sought-after sea route to the East.

For French explorer Jacques Cartier (1491–1557), seeking the trade route to the East was much more than a search for riches. It was a grand adventure, as well as a valuable opportunity to explore new frontiers, claim additional territory for France, and in the process accumulate immense wealth for himself.

By the time Cartier set sail in 1534, the French had already established a presence in North America. As early as 1504, French fishermen looking for "sea silver," as the cod fish was called, were fishing in the waters of Cape Breton, off the coast of Nova Scotia. Enterprising fur traders were also slowly making their way into the interior of what later became known as Canada, while others hunted the "beast of the great teeth," or the walrus. The French, though not formally establishing their claim to territory in North America, certainly had explored, fished, trapped, and hunted there at least three decades before Cartier's first voyage set out in 1534.

Cartier's eye for detail and his natural curiosity enabled him to leave behind an invaluable historical record. Details of his journeys survive through his journals and maps, which are now stored in archives in France and Canada. More than 450 years after Cartier first came to the New World, the details of his travels continue to captivate and instruct readers, providing them with a story of a time when searching the horizon and embarking across the sea meant a journey into the vast unknown.

1
THE MAKING OF
AN EXPLORER

He should be robust and alert, have good sea–legs and be inde–
fatigable . . . He must not be above lending a hand to the work
himself to make the seamen more prompt in their attention . . .
He must be . . . cognizant of everything concerning ship handling.
—Samuel Champlain, as quoted in *The European Discovery of*
America: The Northern Voyages, AD 500–1600

ocated in Brittany, a province in northwestern
France, the coastal town of Saint-Malo has
long been home to the maritime trades. Legend
has it that the town received its name from a sixth-
century Welsh monk who came there hoping to convert the residents to Christianity. For centuries
pirates and other wayfarers found shelter behind the
fortified walls of Saint-Malo. The town also occupied an important place in the history of the
European slave trade. Saint-Malo provided a safe
harbor for French slave ships, which often stopped
there to take on supplies in preparation for the long
journey from West Africa to the French Caribbean.

This watercolor depicts Jacques Cartier as he arrives at Stadacona, Quebec,
in 1534. After stopping at several points along the southern shore of
Labrador, such as Chateau, Greenish Harbour, and Red Bay, Cartier was
disappointed. The land was rough, full of rocks, and lacking soil.

Despite the opportunities to profit from illegal activities, the inhabitants of Saint-Malo also ran a number of legal businesses. They were fearless in protecting their commercial rights and independence, going so far as to rebel against the regional governor in 1590, and declaring their city an independent republic. Their fearlessness, independence, and determination seem to have been inherited by one of the most famous residents of Saint-Malo: explorer Jacques Cartier.

Beyond the year of his birth—1491—historians know little about Cartier's family background or early life. It seems likely that the young Cartier, intrigued by the stories he heard from the sailors and fishermen who found their way to Saint-Malo, was drawn to the sea. Although it is unclear whether members of his family were themselves seafaring men, historians know that by the age of thirteen, Jacques Cartier had decided to become a sailor.

Like many other boys who yearned for adventure on the high seas, Cartier began as a cabin boy, or *mousse* ("mouse" in English). Though details of his specific responsibilities are sketchy, he probably ran errands for the captain and the crew while learning many aspects of seamanship—navigation, map reading, and astronomy—that he later excelled in.

While exciting, seafaring was a difficult and dangerous profession. Despite their youth, cabin boys such as Cartier had to perform many of the same chores as the most seasoned "old salt." If small and agile, for example, they proved the ideal mate to climb the rigging and help set the sails. This task carried severe risks; one unexpected gust of wind or one careless misstep could send a boy plunging to his death on the deck below or tumbling headlong into the sea.

Like other members of the crew, cabin boys shared crowded quarters in the lower decks, which were often dark, sweltering, and foul smelling. No wonder so many seamen slept on deck when the weather cooperated. If living conditions were unhealthy, food was often less than nourishing. Unlike the captain or ship's officers, who often dined on fresh fish as well as fruits and vegetables, crew members had to make do with a biscuit, known as hardtack, and a half-pound of salted meat or fish per day. When available, rice, legumes, such as peas or peanuts, and cheese complemented their diet, which also included a ration of wine. Although it appears that most sailors received enough to eat during a voyage, at least in terms of caloric intake, it was also common for the captains to deprive their men and to sell "excess" supplies for a profit. In addition to a lack of healthy food, seamen—even as late as the nineteenth century—rarely ate without finding that rats, mice, or insects had infested their food. Conditions on shipboard might have been even worse had not most captains been practical men who realized that it was in their best interest to maintain a

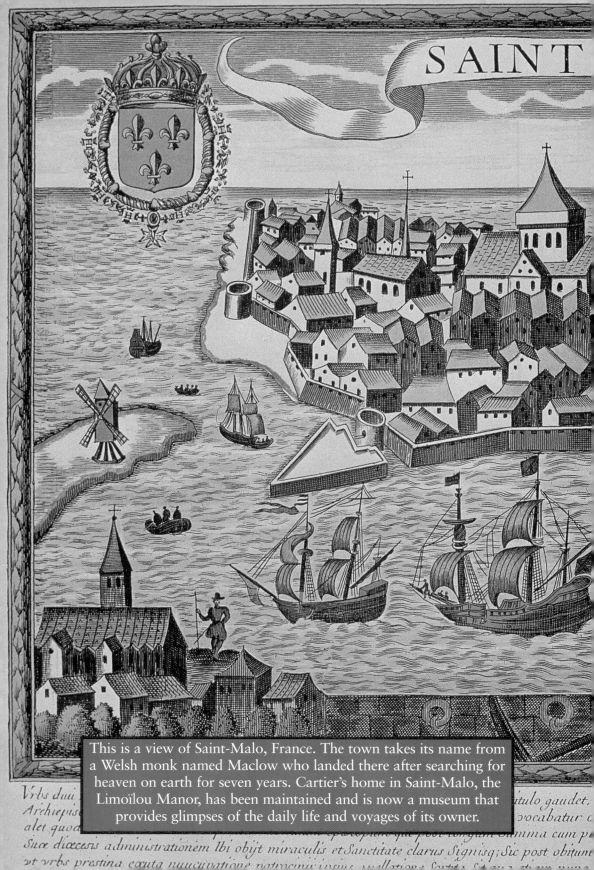

This is a view of Saint-Malo, France. The town takes its name from a Welsh monk named Maclow who landed there after searching for heaven on earth for seven years. Cartier's home in Saint-Malo, the Limoïlou Manor, has been maintained and is now a museum that provides glimpses of the daily life and voyages of its owner.

Vrbs dui, ...titulo gaudet,
Archiepisc... vocabatur
alet quod ...
Suce diœcesis administrationem Ibi obijt miraculis et Sanctitate clarus Signisq; Sic post obitum
vt vrbs prestina, exuta nuucupatione patrocinij insuit, vuallatio...

ALO

Derveaux Edit Col

SAINT MALO *Est vne ville fort Considerable Situeé Sur la Coste de Bretaigne, et presque toutte enuuronneé de la*

Cette ville portoit autrefois le nom d'Alet, quelle n'a quitté que pour prendre celuy d'vn de Ses Euesques qui a pres

ir gouuerné long temps Son Eglise auec vne pieté exemplaire y mourut en odeur de Sainteté. Son Euesché est

rágant de Larcheuesché de Tours et Sestend Sur plus de trois cens Paroisses. Les habitans de cette ville Sont

de Marchandises quils vont querir eux mesme par Mer

relatively well-fed and healthy crew. Otherwise they would not be strong enough to handle the various chores that needed to be done.

Perhaps the greatest threat to sailors was disease. Outbreaks of plague, dysentery (caused by the infestation of the bowels by parasites), and fever could destroy an entire crew within days. At the time, there was little medical knowledge about the transmission of diseases. Although many ships carried a surgeon, he was often more prepared to tend to battle wounds than to combat outbreaks of scurvy (caused by a lack of vitamin C), rickets (caused by a lack of calcium), or dysentery. Constant exposure to the elements, poor diets, tainted or spoiled food, bad drinking water, filthy conditions in which garbage and human waste were not quickly disposed of, the contamination of clothing and beds with lice and other bugs, and the infrequency of bathing combined to make sailors' health questionable and their lives short.

There were even greater dangers to be found at sea. Attacks from roving pirates seeking to steal precious cargoes were a constant threat. So were shipwrecks. A shipwreck could be caused by a variety of things, from war to foul weather. Rocks near a port of call could punch a hole in a vessel's hull. High winds and water could batter a ship into nothing more than planks of wood and cords of rope. Fire, whether caused by an enemy cannon or a careless crewman smoking his pipe, could destroy a ship in no time.

The magnetic compass, seen here, is the oldest instrument for navigation and has been a vital tool for seamen for centuries. The compass allows ships to steer a selected course. By taking bearings of visible objects with a compass, a navigator was able to steer the selected course and also able to fix a ship's position on a chart.

For many sailors, a shipwreck was among the worst things that could happen, for few men survived such a calamity.

Despite these hazards, Jacques Cartier did survive and worked his way up through the ranks. From cabin boy, Cartier became a novice seaman. He then earned recognition as a full-fledged sailor. Early on, Cartier had shown skill as a navigator. There seemed little doubt that one day he would become the master of his own vessel. It was only a matter of time.

In 1520, Cartier returned to Saint-Malo to wed Catherine des Granches, the daughter of the local high constable, a man of considerable reputation and influence. Cartier's marriage into a prominent local family may even have aided his career, enabling him to advance more quickly to the rank of master-pilot than he would otherwise have done.

By 1532, when he was forty-one years old, Jacques Cartier had established himself as a seaman of great skill and daring. No doubt by this time he had heard many tales of voyages to the New World, which must have excited his vivid imagination and his thirst for adventure. So fascinated was he with the notion of traveling to the land beyond the sea that later in 1532, when approached about undertaking a voyage there to explore and claim territory for the kingdom of France, Cartier accepted the offer without hesitation. It was an opportunity that answered his most burning ambitions and his most ardent dreams.

2

A ROYAL COMMISSION

Who seeks the way to win renown
Or flies with wings of high desire;
Who seeks to wear the laurel crown
Or hath the mind that would aspire,
Tell him his native soil eschew,
Tell him go range and seek anew
—Anonymous sixteenth-century English verse

At the beginning of the sixteenth century, France was far behind Portugal and Spain in terms of overseas expansion. While navigators in the employ of Portugal and Spain had already begun to explore and colonize parts of Africa, India, the Far East, and the New World, the French had been occupied fighting and recovering from the Hundred Years' War (1337–1453) against the English. By the sixteenth century, Francis I, the king of France, had no intention of being left farther behind. Inspired by the quest for riches and the possibility of establishing an overseas empire, Francis decided to dispatch French explorers to the New World.

Comment la ville de libodane fut prinse de force par les Anglois Le chapitre

E nuiron quatre Zours apres ce que messire Jehan de hollande et aresse Thomas de persi furent venus en lost du mareschal Et guilz eurent Cheualiers et esquiere auec toutes manieres de gene ordonnez a bon appareil dassault Apres plusieurs euures faites a ce seruans et charpenter de bois vn engien sur roes que on pouoit bien mener a force dhoes

la ou on vouloit Et dedens cellur pouoient bien aiseement Cent archiers et autant de gens dars qui eust voulu mais pour cest assault archiere y entrerent Et auoit on raempli le fosse alendroit ou lengien deuoit estre menes Lors commenca lassault et lengien a aprochier la ville legl aloit a force de boutemens sur roes Et laiane et tout entour estoient archiere bien pourueue de flesches que ilz trauoient a ceulx

English troops capture a French town during the Hundred Years' War between England and France. This is an illumination (a page from text decorated with ornamental designs, miniatures, or lettering) from Jean Froissart's *Chronicles*, an historical account of events in Europe in the fourteenth century. Froissart completed his book in 1400, while this illustrated version was made in 1470.

The French were well aware of the exciting possibilities of exploring new lands that the Portuguese and the Spanish were discovering half a world away. By the beginning of the sixteenth century, fishermen from the French provinces of Normandy and Brittany had sailed into North American waters hoping to profit from the rich fisheries off the coast in the area of what is now Newfoundland. Soon thereafter, the first of many French explorers ventured to North America, hoping not only to find the long-sought Northwest Passage to shorten the route to the Far East, but also to claim land, glory, and wealth for France.

In 1506, the French explorer Jean Denys of Honfleur, a city in the French province of Normandy, sailed along the Atlantic coast from the Strait of Belle Isle to Bonavista, near Newfoundland. Two years later, in 1508, Thomas Aubert from the city of Dieppe, (also located in Normandy), sailed in these same waters and returned home carrying with him the first "Indians," or Native Americans to visit France. Historians believe they were most likely members of the Miawpukek, or Micmac Nation. However beneficial, these efforts fell far short of bringing Francis I the prestige and riches that he sought from the New World.

Apart from wealth and power, Francis had other reasons for seeking a more direct trade route to the East. If successful, he would be in a better position to challenge his long-time rival, Charles V, the king of Spain and Holy Roman Emperor. Relations between the two monarchs had never been cordial, but they had worsened considerably after Charles had been chosen Holy Roman Emperor in 1519 instead of Francis. Between 1521 and 1559 the kingdoms of France and Spain engaged in almost constant warfare.

By the time Charles became king in 1516, Spain had emerged as the dominant power in the New World; by 1550 the Spanish empire encompassed nearly the whole of Mexico and Central and South America, and also included a sizeable portion of what is now the United States.

The Papal Bull of 1493, in which Pope Alexander VI divided the New World between Portugal and Spain, helped to legitimize Spanish claims to this vast territory. This document not only formalized Spanish claims but also forbade any countries besides Spain and Portugal from entering or exploring lands that had been seized by either of those two powers. For those countries, such as France and England, that were interested in exploring the Americas, the papal decree stated that this part of the world now belonged principally to Spain.

A bitter rivalry with the Spanish, who had already made inroads into South America, and a desire for a share of eastern trade profits fueled King Francis's determination to lead France into maritime exploration. This portrait of Francis I is believed to have been painted by Jean Clouet in 1525.

Pope Clement VII (*pictured above*) reversed an earlier decision that favored the Spanish hold over the Americas, opening the way for other countries to explore there.

Francis, however, refused to recognize Pope Alexander's decision. He argued that the pope had no right to divide the world in this manner, and that in order for a country to claim a territory, it had to establish permanent settlements there. Otherwise, the search for land and new commercial opportunities should be open to any country that wished to pursue them. Finally, in 1533, Francis convinced Pope Clement VII—who succeeded to the office of pope in 1523—to amend Alexander's earlier decision. As a result, any territories that the Spanish and Portuguese had discovered were declared to belong to them. Any undiscovered territory, however, was open to exploration by the other world powers.

In the meantime, Francis was busy trying to catch up with his imperial rivals. In 1524, the Italian sailor Giovanni da Verrazano, sailing under the flag of France, started on a journey in search of the fabled Northwest Passage to the Far East. Although unsuccessful in finding the route, Verrazano explored the Atlantic coast of

A Tall Order

Included in the royal commission—a special document issued by the king that Cartier received from Francis I—were his instructions for the voyage. According to this document, Cartier was to "discover certain islands and lands where it was said that a great quantity of gold, and other precious things are to be found." This meant that Cartier was also to continue the search for the Northwest Passage and to claim any riches he might find for the king of France. In addition, the charter recognized Cartier as the *Capitaine et Pilote pour le Roy*, which meant that he was the king's official captain. A pilot in the seafaring culture of Europe was often recognized as a ship's officer, whose rank was equivalent to that of a first mate. Because Cartier was also a senior captain on all his voyages, his rank was that of a naval commodore, one of the highest that can be attained in any navy.

North America from the Carolinas to New York State, and claimed these lands in the name of Francis I. Though it is not proven, historians believe that young Jacques Cartier joined Verrazano on these voyages.

Not discouraged by these early failures, Francis decided to send another expedition to the New World in 1532. Acting upon the recommendation of the bishop of Saint-Malo, Jean Le Veneur, the king met with Jacques Cartier, already a noted seaman and traveler, to inquire if he would be interested in heading the proposed voyage. Francis could not have made a better choice.

By this time, Cartier was an accomplished sailor and a prosperous citizen of Saint-Malo. He was curious about the unknown world and he questioned the common belief that the area now known as Canada was largely uninhabited. Although the promise of acquiring a huge personal fortune was particularly appealing, Cartier also thought that it was his duty to bring Catholicism to the peoples of the earth who had not been exposed to it yet. With these goals in mind, he eagerly accepted the king's offer, and in early 1534, he began making preparations for the voyage.

3

THE NEW WORLD

How Captain Jacques Cartier, Having Set Forth from St.–Malo with Two Ships, Came to the New Land, Called Francis's Land
—Jacques Cartier, The Voyages of Jacques Cartier, c. 1565

On April 20, 1534, a day of clear skies and calm waters, Jacques Cartier wrote in his journal, "When Sir Charles de Mouy . . . Vice-Admiral of France had received the oaths of the captains, masters, and sailors of the vessels, and had made them swear to conduct themselves well and loyally in the King's service . . . we set forth from the harbour and port of St. Malo with two ships." Francis I provided Cartier with two ships—each weighing sixty-one tons—for his 2,000-mile journey across the North Atlantic. A crew of sixty-one sailors manned these vessels. If all went well, both ships and crew would return safely to France in approximately one year.

This 1928 watercolor depicts Jacques Cartier's expedition preparing to leave France. The exploration began in a region encompassing the area between the Strait of Belle Isle and Southern Newfoundland which was already frequented by fishermen from Brittany. After erecting a cross at Saint-Servan on the northern coast of the Gulf, Cartier tacked to the south. He first encountered the Magdalen Islands, and then set course for present-day Prince Edward Island, failing to notice that it was in fact an island.

Aided by good weather, Cartier crossed the Atlantic in record time—only twenty days; it was a remarkably short voyage for the period. Upon arriving in the New World, Cartier sailed northward along the coast of Newfoundland. The waters were icy even though it was May. Cartier and his men came upon a "large number of blocks of ice along the coast," and were forced to sail their ships into a sheltered bay called St. Catherine's Harbor. For ten days, the crew worked on the ship's rigging and prepared smaller boats, called longboats, for use, as they waited for the ice blocks to melt before continuing their journey north up the coast.

On May 21, Cartier recorded the first of many remarkable sights he saw on this voyage. Sailing north from Cape Bonavista, Cartier's ships came upon an amazing place that the French called L'Isle des Oiseaux, or the Isle of Birds, now known as Funk Island. Cartier noted that the island was completely surrounded by cakes of loose ice. Despite this barrier, he sent men in two longboats to explore.

The island was aptly named. Everywhere Cartier and his men looked there were birds of every conceivable color and size: "It is so exceedingly full of birds that one would think they had been stowed there. In the air and round about are a hundred times as many more on the island itself. Some of these birds are as large as geese, being black and white with a beak like a crow's. They are always in the water, not being able to fly in the air."

29

These birds, called apponats, were very fat, and, as the explorers soon learned, they provided a welcome supply of tasty meat. Cartier's men killed as many apponats as they could carry and salted the fresh meat to preserve it for future meals. The sailors also killed one of the many polar bears that swam the icy waters near the island in search of food.

Leaving L'Isle des Oiseaux and continuing northward, Cartier sailed along the bleak and rocky coastline of Labrador. Shifting his course to the southwest, he came upon a waterway called the Strait of Belle Isle, which separates Newfoundland from the Canadian mainland. Many Europeans, including French fishermen who had journeyed to North America, had already taken this route.

That Cartier was aware of these earlier journeys is evident from the entries in his logs. In them, he identified many of the bays, inlets, and islands located along the strait. Cartier even encountered a French fishing boat from La Rochelle (a city on the Atlantic coast of France) that had become lost. He directed his crew into a harbor west of the St. James River, where he had noticed a "harbour [which] is in my opinion one of the best in the world." Cartier was in fact so impressed with the rich soil and excellent location of the site that he named it "Port Jacques Cartier."

By mid June, Cartier had sailed along the entire west coast of Newfoundland, territory that no European had ever explored. Despite poor weather and crude navigational tools, Cartier safely made his way to the southwestern tip of the island and then headed westward toward the Magdalen Islands. Beyond them lay the mainland of Canada and Cartier's dream: the unknown route to the Far East.

Sailing across the gulf, Cartier and his men spotted many beautiful islands that were covered with different types of trees and meadows. Cartier took careful notes on the topography and vegetation they encountered. He also recorded the temperature. In addition, he named many of the islands and rivers that he saw. Periodically, the French explorers encountered the inhabitants of these islands. Once, when Cartier and his men were near an area they called the Savage Cape, a man emerged from the woods and signaled the explorers to come ashore. Cartier wrote in his journal, "We began to row towards him, but when he saw us returning, he started to run away and to flee before us. We landed . . . and placed a knife and a woolen girdle on a branch and returned to our ships."

On a hot and humid July 4, 1534, Cartier and his men landed at a place that they had named Miscou Point, located at the southern opening of a large bay, which Cartier called

In this illustration by Henry Sandham for *The Romance of Canada*, Cartier is shown scaring away Micmac Indians with cannons in 1535. His ships had anchored near a bay where wood and water were plentiful. There, Cartier's men encountered the Micmac, who had traveled there to hunt seals. However, in reality, the incident with the cannon took place on board Cartier's ship.

Chaleur Bay, which means "Warm Bay." Struck by the beauty of the land, which included glistening ponds and lush forests, Cartier wrote in his journal about the various types of trees, paying special attention to the cedar and spruce, both of which became important materials in the manufacture of ship masts. This land was called the Gaspé Peninsula, and is now known as New Brunswick.

Two days later, on July 6, Cartier's ships dropped anchor in a small cove along the north shore of Chaleur Bay. Cartier and some of his men boarded one of the longboats and set out to explore the area. A short distance from their boats, they noticed forty to fifty bark canoes filled with Micmac Indians who were crossing from the opposite side of the bay. The Indians were shouting and holding out animal skins on sticks in the hopes of trading them with the French. They gestured for Cartier and his men to join them. Outnumbered and uncertain about the Indians' intentions, Cartier ordered his men to return to the safety of their ships. Some of the Indians followed. Cartier waved them away, but they only paddled harder toward the French longboats. Soon the Micmac Indians surrounded them and, fearing an attack, Cartier ordered his men to fire the two small cannons they had brought with them. The explosions frightened the Micmac and they scattered hurriedly. The diversion gave Cartier and his men enough time to reach their vessels.

Cartier encounters Indians on the Saint Louis River in this painting by Théodore Grudin. The Iroquois lived near the present site of Quebec City in a settlement called Stadacona. At that time, Iroquoian villages dominated the St. Lawrence area from the Gaspé Peninsula to Lake Ontario.

Meanwhile, it was becoming apparent to Cartier that locating the Northwest Passage would not be as simple as he had hoped. However, everywhere he looked there were inlets and islands waiting to be explored. With any luck, one of them might hold the key to a shorter, faster, and cheaper route to the East.

The day after their first encounter with the Micmac Indians, another group of Micmac, who had brought furs to trade, signaled to the French ships. Feeling reasonably assured that they meant no harm, Cartier welcomed them. Once again, Cartier and some of his men boarded a longboat and set off for shore where the Micmac were waiting. To show that they came in peace, the French offered the Indians beads and other trading goods, such as knives, mirrors, needles, and tiny tin bells, as well as a bright red cap, to present to their chief. The Micmac, according to Cartier in his journal, made a great show of receiving their new treasures, passing them from person to person, dancing, even throwing water over their heads. Noting the pleasure they took in the gifts, Cartier was sure that the Micmac would return to trade with the French.

Regardless, Cartier didn't stay in Chaleur Bay for long. On July 8, the French weighed anchor and, despite stormy weather, set sail to the north toward the Gaspé Passage. Arriving at the northeastern point of the peninsula, Cartier and his men encountered another group of Indians, whom historians believe were members of a group known as the Stadaconans. Though the Stadaconans were considered part of a larger group known as the St. Lawrence Iroquois, they were not members of the Iroquois confederacy. The Stadaconans were quite different from the Micmacs. According to Cartier's journal, not only did they speak a completely different language, but they ate their meat and fish almost raw. Cartier noted in his journal that:

This people may well be called savage; for they are the sorriest folk there can be in the world . . . They go quite naked, except for a small skin . . . and for a few skins which they throw over their shoulders . . . They have their heads shaved all around in circles, except for a tuft on the top of the head, which they leave long like a horse's tail.

Cartier also observed that the Stadaconans knew little about trading and were perfectly happy to receive the sometimes cheap offerings that the French presented. The Stadaconans, however, stole from the Frenchmen, seeming to believe, as Cartier suggested, that any unused article was free for the taking. Despite this potentially explosive misunderstanding, Cartier was more than willing to trade, and offered the Stadaconans bells, combs, and other items in exchange for furs and fish.

Cartier and his men erect a cross in Stadacona in 1534. Initially the Stadaconans trusted the French explorers. But relations with the Indians were tarnished when Cartier claimed possession of the territory on July 24. The thirty-foot cross he erected at Pointe-Penouille seemed improper to Donnacona, the Stadaconan chief. Fearful of a confrontation, Cartier lied and claimed that the cross was an insignificant landmark.

On July 24, approximately two weeks after they had landed on the Gaspé Peninsula, the French constructed a giant wooden cross that rose to a height of thirty feet. Directly beneath the crossbar they placed a small plaque decorated with three fleurs-de-lys, the three-petaled lily flowers that were the symbol of the French king. The French wrote "LONG LIVE THE KING OF FRANCE" on the plaque in large letters. Standing at the entrance to the harbor, with a small band of Stadaconans observing them, Cartier and his men hoisted the cross and anchored it into the ground. They then joined hands and knelt in prayer, claiming the land in the name of France and her king.

This was not the first time a cross had been raised on Canadian soil. Cartier's records show that at least eleven crosses of different sizes were erected on land that Cartier visited. But Cartier's cross was the largest to be raised thus far. Unlike the other crosses, which were used as guideposts for navigators, Cartier's cross was more of a symbol—a formal declaration that the French now owned the land he had discovered.

The Stadaconan chief, Donnacona, also realized that Cartier's actions represented much more than a series of trading exchanges, and that the large cross was not just a navigational tool for the French. Accompanied by his three sons, Donnacona set out to visit Cartier's ship. While Cartier watched, Donnacona—sitting in his canoe and dressed in an old black bearskin—angrily gestured and pointed, making it clear that he wanted the French to remove the cross from land that belonged to his people.

Instead of trying to scare the chief away, Cartier held up an ax to the chief, indicating that he would trade it for one of Donnacona's animal

Two Visitors to France

Donnacona's sons went with Cartier to France, where in a short time they learned enough French to enable them to act as translators and interpreters for Cartier when he returned to the New World. It was in this capacity that the two served Cartier on his next voyage to North America in 1535. As he had promised, Cartier returned Taignoagny and Domagaya to their village, much to their father's delight. Although they helped Cartier during his second voyage, political tensions between Donnacona and a rival prompted Cartier to leave Taignoagny and Domagaya with their father. Cartier thought it best to leave the sons with their father when he departed Stadacona because of long-standing tensions between Donnacona and the chief of the Hochelaga.

This is a detail from a map by Descaliers drawn in 1536 or 1542. It shows Cartier and his followers in Canada. Maps full of illustrations and text were popular from the thirteenth to sixteenth centuries, as they recorded the accumulated experience and wisdom of generations of Mediterranean seamen.

skins. When the chief held out his hand to reach for the ax, some of Cartier's men, (who were traveling behind Donnacona's canoe in a dinghy, or small boat), surrounded the canoe and politely gestured for the chief and his sons to board the ship. Once on board, Cartier presented his visitors with large amounts of food and drink and, using gestures and what little Iroquois he could speak, explained that the cross was nothing but a landmark for other ships that might sail into the area. Cartier also told Donnacona that he would be journeying back to France and he would return with even finer goods to trade. Cartier then asked the chief to allow two of his sons, Taignoagny and Domagaya, to accompany him to France. With Cartier's promise that the boys would be well treated and eventually returned home, Donnacona reluctantly agreed.

Cartier presented Taignoagny and Domagaya with shirts and red caps, and placed small brass chains around their necks. Cartier presented an ax and two knives to each of the other visitors. Later that day, while Cartier and his men prepared to leave the bay, six canoes filled with Stadaconans paddled up to the ships to say goodbye to Taignoagny and Domagaya. They also promised Cartier that the cross would be allowed to stand.

The following morning Cartier set sail for the northeast. Shortly thereafter, the expedition came upon a large island, now known as Anticosti Island, near the entrance to the St. Lawrence River. Cartier partially explored the island, following the shoreline until he reached a narrow strait that today bears his name and which separates the island from the coast of Quebec. Meanwhile, supplies were running low and it was almost the end of summer; cold weather was on its way. Winter storms would make sea travel dangerous, and the thought of remaining in a strange country, with the possibility of being stranded, was not appealing. As much as he believed he was on the verge of discovering the northwest route to the East, Cartier decided it was wiser to return to France. On August 5, 1534, he and his men guided their vessels eastward and made for home.

4

AN AMAZING
DISCOVERY

You will learn and hear of . . . the great river which flows
through and . . . which is without comparison the largest river
that is known to have ever been seen.
　　　　　　　　　—Jacques Cartier, "Cartier's Second Voyage,"
　　　　　　　　　　　　　　　　The Voyages of Jacques Cartier

A lthough he had failed to find the route to the East, or to bring back the gold and precious gems he had promised, Cartier nonetheless enjoyed a hero's welcome when he returned to Saint-Malo on September 5, 1534. Because of his exceptional navigational abilities and his keen leadership, he had also not lost a vessel or a single crewman on the voyage.

Cartier maintained a detailed journal recording the places and things he encountered. In the process he made a major contribution to Canadian toponymy, mainly by recording the names of locations that he visited during his explorations. He also named many sites and features himself, including the St. Lawrence River and Montreal.

When he met with Francis I, Cartier stressed his belief that a route to the Far East was only a short distance from where he had sailed. Clearly, neither Cartier nor the king had any idea of the size of the country Cartier had just explored. Regardless, the king was impressed enough with Cartier's initial reports to offer him another commission, which included a promotion for Cartier to the rank of master pilot, three ships, a crew of 110 men, and a stipend of 3,000 livres to cover expenses.

Francis indicated that Cartier was to explore the gulf thoroughly and find the precious metals and jewels the king so desperately hoped for. In addition, Cartier was charged with carrying out what was known as the Great Commission, which was to convert the Indian tribes to the Roman Catholic faith. On his second voyage to the New World, Cartier planned to stay the winter in North America, though he had no intention of setting up a permanent French settlement. Cartier and his men would be the first Europeans to spend an extended period of time in North America since the Vikings ventured to those shores centuries before.

On May 19, 1535, Cartier's three ships set out from the harbor at Saint-Malo. On board *La Grande Hermine*, the largest of the three ships, which weighed over 120 tons, was Commander Cartier, along with a few members of the royal court. The other

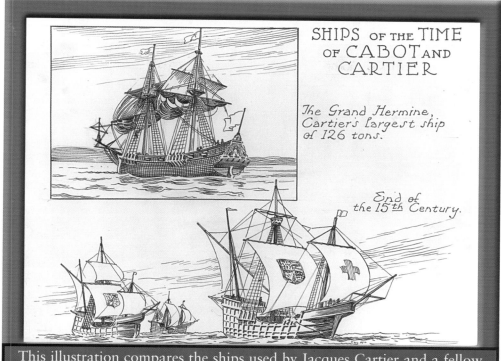

SHIPS OF THE TIME OF CABOT AND CARTIER

The Grand Hermine, Cartier's largest ship of 126 tons.

End of the 15th Century.

This illustration compares the ships used by Jacques Cartier and a fellow explorer, Italian sailor Giovanni Caboto, better known as John Cabot. Cabot sailed from Bristol, England, to North America with a grant from King Henry VII to explore the possibility of a northwestern route to Asia. Cabot's ship on his first journey weighed only fifty tons, compared to Cartier's *La Grande Hermine*, which weighed 126 tons.

two vessels traveling in Cartier's flotilla were much smaller: *La Petite Hermine* weighed about sixty tons and *l'Emerillon*, the smallest of the three, weighed only forty tons. Accompanying Cartier on this voyage were 112 men, including a dozen of his relatives as well as carpenters, a doctor, and his crew of sailors and officers. To protect the flotilla from attack by the Spanish or pirates, Cartier had ordered *La Grande Hermine* fitted with twelve guns.

Riding on horseback and surrounded by courtiers, King Francis I receives Jacques Cartier at Fontainbleu and listens to his account of his discoveries. This oil painting by Frank Craig depicts Scene II from the First Pageant of the Historical Pageants on the Plains of Abraham, National Celebration of Quebec, held there in 1908. It is one of six paintings that Craig produced as illustrations for the *King's Book of Quebec*, published in 1911.

Unfortunately, the good weather that had aided Cartier on his first journey did not accompany him on his second. Instead, terrible storms battered the French throughout the entire Atlantic crossing. On June 25, the ships became separated from each other in a storm and remained out of contact until July 7, when all three met at the Isle of Birds near Newfoundland, some fifty days after sailing from Saint-Malo.

After taking on almost two boatloads of the tasty apponat birds to add to their stores, the French pushed on toward Anticosti Island. On August 8, Cartier and his ships had reached the

An Amazing Sight

One interesting diversion for Cartier and his men was the unusual fish that they saw on their journeys. Writing in his journal, Cartier noted that the creatures were as large as porpoises but had no fins. They were "similar to greyhounds about the body and head," he wrote, and were "as white as snow," without spots. "Of these there are a very large number in this river," he concluded. "The people of the country call them *Adhothuys* and told us they are very good to eat." The "fish" that Cartier described were actually white whales, also known as Beluga whales.

mouth of a great river, whose distance from north to south alone spanned almost eighty miles. Cartier called the river "la Grande Rivière," or "the big river." As that day was the feast day of St. Lawrence, Cartier named a harbor near the mouth of the river in honor of the saint. Even though Cartier always referred to the river as la Grande Rivière, future explorers of the area would apply the name "St. Lawrence" to the entire river. His guides, Domagaya and Taignoagny, assured Cartier that this waterway marked the beginning of the passage to a kingdom of great wealth. According to an early legend, this kingdom was inhabited by white blond men, rich with gold and furs, in a place they called Saguenay. As Cartier noted in his journal:

> *Our savages told us that this was the beginning of the Saguenay and of the inhabited region, and that thence came the copper called caigneldaze . . . The two savages assured us that this was the way to the mouth of the great river of Hockelaga and the route towards Canada.*

This kingdom, was located in a land they called Canada. The two brothers also told Cartier that no one had ever reached the end of the great river, which grew narrower the farther one traveled. Cartier was thrilled, believing he had at last found the Northwest Passage to the East.

For the next several days, Cartier explored the various islands and inlets of the St. Lawrence. He and his men made careful notes of everything they saw, from the lush forests on the land to the water teeming with fish. Cartier also measured the distances between the islands and the mainland as well as calculated the depth of the water. While the French were greatly impressed with what they found, they nevertheless sensed a growing uneasiness about what lay in store for them as they continued their journey into uncharted territory.

On September 1, 1535, Cartier set sail in search of Saguenay. His ships battled swift and dangerous currents that threatened to send them into nearby sandbars or crashing into the jagged rocks. Cartier noticed that as the expedition moved farther upriver away from the Atlantic Ocean, the St. Lawrence gradually turned from saltwater to freshwater. By September 6, after having traveled forty-five miles, Cartier reached a small island, which he named Coudres Island. He pushed on for another twenty miles and came to a series of islands that his Indian guides told him marked the beginning of the territory Cartier described as Canada. In actuality, Cartier's guides called the area *kanata*, which referred to the village of Stadacona. "Kanata" was simply the Iroquoian word for "village" or "settlement." But for want of another name, Cartier used "Canada" in referring to the entire area he would explore.

After dropping anchor, Cartier and several of his men made their way ashore, where they encountered a group of Iroquois Indians and members of Chief Donnacona's tribe. Upon seeing the French, the Indians ran away. But, with the help of Domagaya and Taignoagny, Cartier explained who he was. Listening to the brothers, the Indians welcomed their visitors and brought them food. In return, Cartier offered his hosts several small trinkets as gifts of thanks for their hospitality before he and his men returned to their ships.

The following day, Chief Donnacona, accompanied by several of his warriors, came to Cartier's ship. He formally welcomed Cartier and eagerly embraced his sons. Cartier ordered that bread and wine be brought to the chief and his men. After the Indians finished eating, they returned to their village.

Later that same day Cartier and some of his men journeyed in their longboats up the St. Lawrence until they arrived at a fork in the river. Finding a small harbor, Cartier decided that all three ships should be brought to the site, where their crews could rest and replenish their stores. To the delight and surprise of the French, the residents of nearby Stadacona (now the site of Quebec City), welcomed them. As it turned out, they had come across the home of Donnacona.

Discussing his journey with Donnacona, Cartier told him that he planned to sail farther up the river to a place known as

55

After days of sailing up the St. Lawrence River, Cartier came across Hochelaga, a village occupied by the Hochelaga tribespeople. This is a plan of the village showing the circular layout of the village, the wooden fence surrounding it, and the large dwellings enclosed within.

MONTE REAL

LA TERRA DE HOCHELAGA
NELLA NOVA FRANCIA.

A. Porta della Terra Hochelaga.
B. Strada principale, che va alla piazza.
C. Piazza.
D. Casa del Re Agouhana.
E. La Corte della casa del Re, & il suo fuoco.
F. Vna delle dieci strade della Città.
G. Vna delle case priuate.
H. Corte con il fuoco, doue si cucina.
I. Spacio tra le case, & la Città, doue si puo andare attorno.
K. L'ordimento, che tiene le tauole della cinta della Città, che è fatta in luogo di mure.
L. Tauoloni congionti di fuora della città.
M. Spacio di fuora al circuito della Città.
N. Tauole congionte di dentro via il circuito della Città.
O. Corridor doue stanno gli huomini per diffesa della Città.
P. Parapetto doue stanno gli huomini alla diffesa.
Q. Il vacuo che è tra vna tauola, & l'altra, doue è l'ordimento che tien le tauole.
R. Indiani, & Indiane, & putti che sono di fuori della Città p vedere li Francesi.
S. Francesi che entrono nella Città, & che toccano la mano alli Indiani, che erano di fuori della Città appresso al fuoco, & si fanno carezze.
T. La Scala che va su'l Corridor.

Hochelaga in search of the kingdom of Saguenay. Donnacona became annoyed. He said there was nothing upstream worth seeing, and that Cartier would be better off staying with him in Stadacona. The chief was also angered at the possibility that Cartier might begin trading with other tribes. But Cartier explained that he had promised his "chief" that he would travel as far up the river as possible. Donnacona became even more agitated and vexed. He hinted that if Cartier went farther, he would not permit his sons to accompany him. Despite laying a great feast for the French and giving two small boys and a young girl to Cartier as gifts, Donnacona could not persuade him to change his mind.

Growing Concerns

During his visit at Stadacona, Cartier noticed a change in Donnacona. Through his interpreters, Cartier learned that Donnacona was angry that Cartier's men carried guns. According to Cartier's journal, "Donnacona was vexed that the Captain and his people carried so many weapons when they on their side carried none." To this objection Cartier replied that "for all Donnacona's grief, he would not cease to carry [guns] since such was the custom in France." Nothing more was said of the incident, but afterward Cartier became more cautious in his dealings with the chief.

Donnacona would not give up. The day before Cartier intended to leave, three men arrived in a canoe dressed in dog skins, their own skin blackened and wearing horns on their heads. Drawing close to the ship, one of the "devils" shouted at Cartier. Shortly afterward, Domagaya and Taignoagny came to Cartier, greatly agitated, explaining that three devils—messengers from their god, Cudouagny—had come to warn Cartier that if he went ahead with his westward journey he would encounter so much snow and ice that he and his crew would perish.

Upon hearing this warning, Cartier and his men began to laugh, saying that the Frenchmen's god would protect them from the cold weather. Domagaya and Taignoagny returned to the village to tell Donnacona of Cartier's response. Donnacona then made a great show of telling Cartier that this episode had been a joke and that it was meant in no way to deter him from his travels. He remained unwilling to let Cartier take his two sons on this leg of the journey, however. Tired of the Indians' antics, Cartier agreed. It was not until he reached Hochelaga that Cartier learned of the real reasons for Donnacona's attempts to stop him from going.

On September 19, Cartier left for Hochelaga, aboard the *l'Emerillon*. Almost two weeks later, on October 2, the ship arrived safely. There, Cartier found a thriving Hochelagan

This map of Hochelaga, the site of Montreal in Marc Lescarbot's *Histoire de la Nouvelle-France*, is from 1609. Lescarbot was a French lawyer who traveled with the French explorers Jean de Poutrincourt and Samuel de Champlain and wrote a detailed book upon his return. He introduced Christianity to the Indians and helped the settlers by building a mill to process wheat, a still to produce tar, and ovens for making charcoal.

village located at the foot of a hill, which he later christened Mont Réal, or "Mount Royal," and which today is the site of Montreal. Cartier noted that the village was surrounded by a large, circular wooden fence, with several long houses situated inside. Later, when he inspected these dwellings, he found them to be almost 100 feet long. The interiors consisted of several rooms, with a family residing in each.

When they saw the French longboats approaching the shore, almost 1,000 of the village residents came to greet Cartier and his men, bringing gifts of food, including cornbread, which they threw into the French boats. According to Cartier's journal, the Hochelagans thought that Cartier was a god who had special healing powers. Because of this, they brought him their sick to heal. For five days the residents of Hochelaga feasted and celebrated. Among many of the gifts they presented was tobacco, which the Indians smoked in long pipes. While the Hochelagans believed that smoke kept them in good health, Cartier didn't like the taste of tobacco, and noted that it was as if "one had taken powdered pepper, it is so hot."

Cartier persuaded the Hochelagans to stop celebrating his arrival long enough to allow him to explore the mountain. From this vantage point Cartier saw large rapids at the junction of the St. Lawrence and Ottawa

Rivers, which he called Rapides de Lachine, or the Chinese Rapids, since he believed China lay just beyond them. To his great disappointment, however, Cartier realized that he had gone as far as he could with his ship. The dangerous Rapides de Lachine would permit no further passage upriver.

In talking with his hosts, Cartier learned that they, too, had heard of the fabled kingdom of Saguenay, which they believed to be located somewhere northwest of Hochelaga. They spoke of a fierce group of "bad people" who were known for their courage and savagery in battle. They also told Cartier of the great inland seas that he could reach through the nearby rivers. Little did Cartier and his men realize that the bodies of water to which the Hochelagans referred were the Great Lakes.

During his stay at Hochelaga, Cartier gradually came to realize that the chief of the village was a more powerful leader among the St. Lawrence Iroquois than was Donnacona. It was no wonder that Donnacona had wished to discourage the French from sailing upriver. He did not want them to travel to Hochelaga and possibly become the allies and trading partners of his rival.

While in Hochelaga, Cartier began to carry out his duty of converting the Indians to Christianity. He read to them from the Bible and gave them "Jesuit rings"—tiny silver rings decorated with Christian symbols such as crosses. To the Indians' delight, Cartier and his men also played songs for them on the instruments they had brought.

On October 5, Cartier and his men set out on their return journey to Stadacona, where his two other ships and the rest of his crew awaited them. He and his men had traveled almost 500 miles since entering the St. Lawrence, but Cartier had still not found the Northwest Passage. The chill of autumn was already in the air by the time Cartier left Hochelaga, and he did not want to waste any time preparing for winter, which he assumed would be similar to those he had known in France. Cartier's assumption was the first of many costly mistakes he would make during the next several months.

5

THE DEADLY WINTER

In the month of December . . . the sickness broke out among us accompanied by most marvelous and extraordinary symptoms.
—Jaques Cartier, "Cartier's Second Voyage, 1535–1536,"
The Voyages of Jacques Cartier

On Monday, October 11, 1535, Cartier and his party returned to St. Croix, where they had left their comrades. According to Cartier's journal, the men who stayed behind "had built a fort in front of the ships, enclosed on all sides with large wooden logs planted upright and joined one to another." To add to the protection that the fortification provided, he had ordered his men to line up their cannons, which they aimed in different directions.

This first page of a facsimile list of Cartier's crew was taken from James P. Baxter's book *A Memoir of Jacques Cartier*, published in 1906. On his first journey, Cartier had 161 crew members; by the third voyage, he had more than 1,000 people traveling with him.

COLLATERAL DOCUMENTS

FACSIMILE OF THE ROLL OF THE CREW OF JACQUES CARTIER,
PRESERVED IN THE ARCHIVES OF ST. MALO

(A TRANSLATION APPEARS ON PAGES 307–310)

1 L'insertion des M^e compaignions mariniers et pilotes s'ensuyuent.

The day after Cartier's return, Donnacona arrived to speak with him and invited Cartier to visit the village the following day. Cartier was greeted with a joyous welcome. In return, Cartier presented gifts to everyone, much to the Indians' delight. Meanwhile, Cartier's men continued to stockpile supplies. They were well prepared for what Cartier believed would be a short and mild winter.

Noting on the map that the region was a few degrees south of Paris, Cartier assumed that the winters would be like those in France. Unfortunately, by the time he realized the enormity of this error, it was too late for the French to do anything but shield themselves as best they could against the harsh conditions. To the astonishment of Cartier and his men, the snow began to fall early and it kept on falling. When the ice froze their ships on the river, they began to feel trapped.

In his icy prison, Cartier occupied himself by observing and recording the wintertime activities of the Stadaconans. Cartier visited regularly with Donnacona and heard wonderful stories about the great kingdom of Saguenay and its fabulous riches. Donnacona also told Cartier that in the kingdom there were white men like the French who wore only woolen garments, as well as terrible one-legged creatures. Cartier noted the details of each story carefully, hoping that his host was telling the truth.

Cartier met different North American tribes during his travels throughout the St. Lawrence region. Though he tried to learn their languages and customs, he never regarded them as more than savages, or "red-skins," who were only useful as guides to explore the land and uncover natural resources to exploit.

To remain on Cartier's good side and to persuade the French not to establish contacts with other Indian groups, Donnacona permitted three small Stadaconan children to stay with the French at the fort. Yet despite goodwill on both sides, as the harsh Canadian winter wore on, relations between the French and the Stadaconan also turned cold. Although both continued to treat the other with respect, a number of incidents threatened the safety of the French and the Stadaconans alike. Donnacona's two sons, Taignoagny and Domagaya, were beginning to turn the Indian community against the French by telling them that the goods the French had brought to trade were worthless. To complicate matters, when Donnacona asked Cartier to return to the village the children he had given the Frenchman as gifts, Cartier refused, explaining that he intended to take them back to France. Cartier was concerned. He could not afford to anger the Stadaconans because his supply of food was running low; by December the French had completely run out of fresh meat. The survival of his men, Cartier reasoned, might well depend on the goodwill of Donnacona and his people.

As it turned out, circumstances were against him. In late December, Cartier received word from the village that a number of Indians had become quite ill. More than fifty had already died. Upon hearing this news, Cartier refused to go the village or to allow any of the Stadaconans to visit the fort. His insistence further strained relations. Cartier wanted to isolate his men from whatever disease was ravaging the Indian village, but it was already too late. Several of Cartier's men also became deathly ill with scurvy.

So widespread was the outbreak that by the middle of February 1536, not more than ten of the original 110-member crew were in good health. Eight Frenchmen had already died, and another fifty were close to death. Concerned about what might be causing the illness, Cartier resorted to the uncommon practice of ordering an autopsy of one of the dead in an effort to learn more about the disease that was wiping out his men.

Soon after, Cartier noticed that Domagaya, who, like his own men, had been sick with scurvy, was walking about. Curious, Cartier asked him to come to the fort so that he might learn how he had been cured. When his visitor arrived, he told Cartier his illness had gone away after drinking broth made from the bark and needles of the white cedar tree. Cartier asked

A Deadly Disease

Scurvy is caused by a lack of vitamin C, which is found in fresh fruits and vegetables. In his journals, Cartier described in great detail the horrible symptoms of the strange disease: "Some [men] lost all their strength, their legs became swollen and inflamed, while the sinews [muscles] contracted and turned black as coal. In other cases the legs were found blotched with purple-colored blood. Then the disease would mount to the hips, thighs, shoulders, arms and neck. And all had their mouths so tainted that the gums rotted away down to the roots of the teeth which nearly all fell out."

The Stadaconans showed Cartier the healing powers of cedar tea, which they used to cure scurvy. Cedar bark is a rich source of ascorbic acid, or vitamin C, the vitamin whose deficiency causes scurvy.

how the tea was made and where he might find this tree. Two Stadaconan women came from the village and showed Cartier where to gather the necessary ingredients. Together, the three brought back several branches. The women then showed Cartier how to grind the bark and needles to make the tea. At first, Cartier's men would have nothing to do with the bad-tasting stuff. Eventually, a few agreed to try it and found that after drinking they began to feel better almost immediately. Cartier later reported in his

A Good Story

Cartier did not fully realize that Donnacona was simply telling his stories for Cartier's pleasure. In Native American culture, storytelling is a great art and a good storyteller is highly regarded. Native Americans, in this case, the Stadaconans, liked to please their guests by telling them what-ever they wanted to hear. In weaving his fanciful tales of the kingdom of Saguenay, Donnacona not only continued to encourage Cartier's dream of finding a route to the East; he also unwittingly contributed to his own kidnapping.

Unfortunately, the taking of Donnacona and the other Indians from their homes severely strained relations between the French and Native Americans for many years.

journal that several of the men who a week earlier had been near death were now recovering and hoped to be out of bed soon. In the end, all the men who took the cure did recover, but not before scurvy claimed almost one-quarter of Cartier's crew, leaving him with only eighty-five men to sail back to France.

By the time spring arrived in May, Cartier was already busy making plans for the return voyage. Because so many of his crew had died, Cartier decided to break up *La Petite Hermine* and return home in the two remaining ships. Cartier noted in his journal that the Indians scavenged through the ruins of the ship looking for nails in the abandoned and broken pieces. He also made another decision that had severe consequences for many years to come. If the kingdom of Saguenay did in fact exist, Cartier reasoned, who better to tell Francis I about it than the man who had told Cartier himself?

On May 5, 1536, Donnacona, accompanied by his two sons and two other Indians, boarded Cartier's ship, despite Taignoagny having warned his father not to do so under any circumstances. Once they were on board, the French took Donnacona and his party into custody. By nightfall, a large number of Donnacona's people had come to the ships crying and demanding the release of their leader. Their wailing and shouting kept up all night and well into

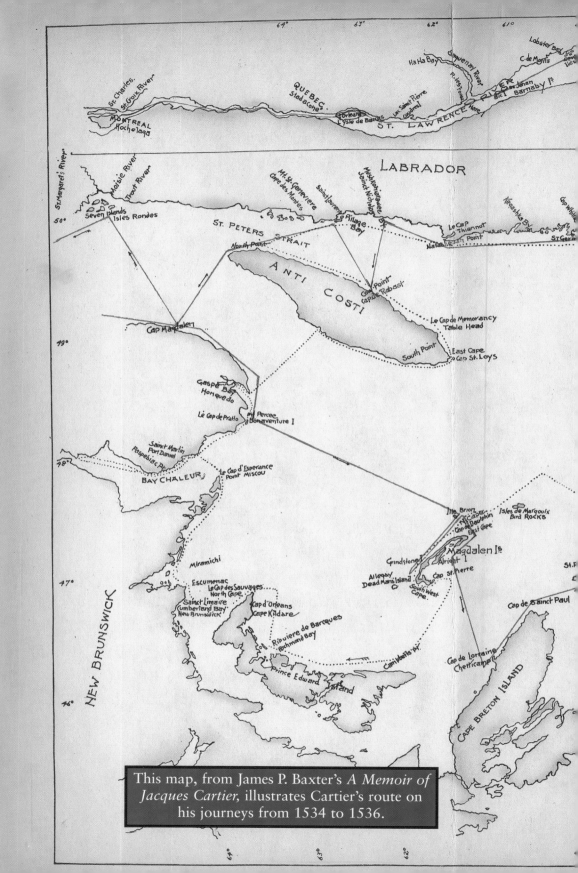

This map, from James P. Baxter's *A Memoir of Jacques Cartier*, illustrates Cartier's route on his journeys from 1534 to 1536.

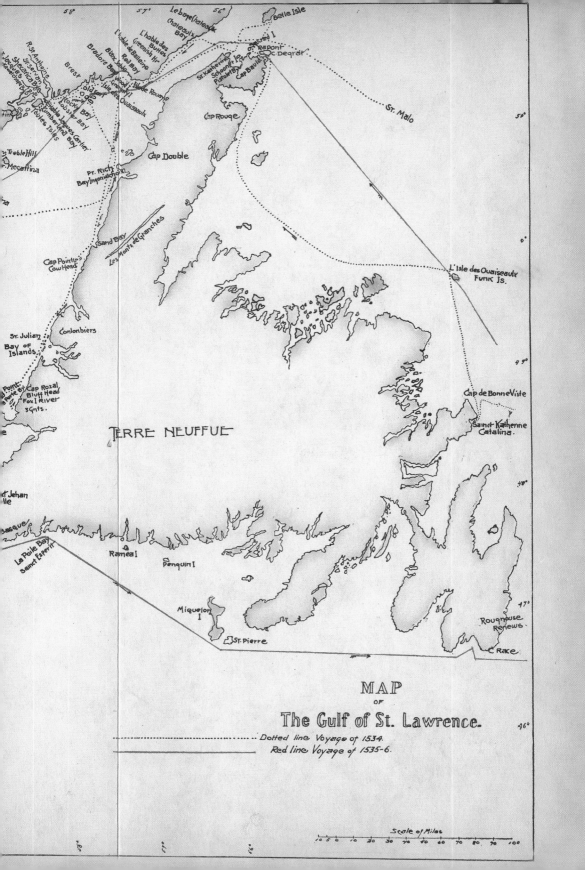

MAP
OF
The Gulf of St. Lawrence.

·············· Dotted line Voyage of 1534.
————————— Red line Voyage of 1535-6.

Scale of Miles

the next morning, until Cartier at last told the people that their leader would speak to them. In the meantime, Cartier had explained to Donnacona that he was taking him to meet the king of France and that in a year he would be allowed to return to his home. Donnacona agreed to leave with Cartier, and he said good-bye to his people.

By May 6, Cartier and his men were on their way back to France after having been gone almost twelve months. In that time, the French had traveled up an unknown river and claimed a great deal of territory in the name of their king. But Cartier was returning with no gold or precious stones to display before the envious courts of Europe, nor had he discovered in the New World any great empires to conquer like those in the south that had fallen under the sway of the hated Spanish.

6

THE ROBERVAL EXPEDITION

Yet he resolved to send the sayd Cartier his pilot thither againe . . . [to] discover more then was done before . . . and attaine if it was possible unto the knowledge of the Countrey of Saguenay.

—Jacques Cartier, "Cartier's Third Voyage, 1541,"
The Voyages of Jacques Cartier

On his return voyage to France, Cartier made an important geographical discovery. He realized that the Magdalen Islands, which he had visited during his first voyage to North America, were not part of the Canadian mainland as he had originally thought. Because of this, Cartier redirected the course of his ships. Instead of traveling north to sail through the Strait of Belle Isle, the French traveled through the strait located between Newfoundland and what is now Cape Breton, Nova Scotia. In doing so, he became the first Frenchman ever to take this route.

Jacques Cartier *(left)* speaks with Jean-François de la Rocque de Roberval. War in Europe had prevented Francis I from sending another expedition to Canada until 1541. This time, to secure French title against the counterclaims of Spain, Francis I commissioned Roberval, a nobleman, to establish a colony in the lands discovered by Cartier.

The rest of the return voyage was uneventful, and finally, on July 16, 1536, Cartier and his two ships sailed into Saint-Malo. Unfortunately, during his absence tensions between France and Spain had worsened and it was only a matter of time before war broke out. If France went to war with Spain, there would be no money for additional trips to North America in the near future. Under the circumstances, it also took months for Cartier to get an audience with the king. To make matters worse, one of Cartier's most influential supporters, Admiral Brion-Cabot, was no longer in the king's favor. With tensions mounting with Spain abroad and his own loss of support at home, Cartier grew concerned that his chances for receiving another commission from the king were slipping away, even though the king recognized Cartier as his "pilot in the western fleet."

By 1538, the war with Spain had ended with the Treaty of Nice. It was nearly two years before Cartier received his next commission from Francis I to undertake a third voyage. Finally, in October 1540, Cartier learned that he had been appointed captain general of a third voyage to North America. In addition, the king furnished him with a handsome sum to outfit ten ships for the journey, six of which Cartier would command. Accompanying Cartier were a crew and passengers of more than 1,000 persons. That fall, Cartier busily prepared his ships and crew for the upcoming voyage.

Francis ordered Cartier to stop looking for the route to China, and instead, to concentrate his efforts on finding the kingdom of Saguenay and its riches. Francis also decided to settle Frenchmen in the New World, and he sent colonists to establish a permanent French settlement in Canada to enforce France's claim over it. Because volunteers were hard to find for such a venture, French officials searched local prisons in an attempt to find potential colonists.

Then in January 1541, Cartier received a piece of unwelcome news. Without warning or explanation Francis I changed his plans. Instead of Cartier leading the expedition, the king appointed Jean-François de la Rocque de Roberval, a member of the French nobility, as the commanding officer and governor of the French colony to be established in Canada. Francis ordered all of the travelers, including Cartier, to swear an oath of loyalty to Roberval. Although Cartier remained in charge of all matters pertaining to the voyage itself, the king had removed him from control of the expedition. Whatever he may have thought or expressed privately about the king's actions, Cartier was careful enough to have neither said anything publicly nor recorded anything in his journal.

This etching shows Cartier *(standing)* and his crew on the third voyage. Cartier traveled with six ships, 400 sailors, 300 soldiers, tradesmen, women, and livestock.

Once the six ships were loaded with enough provisions to last for two years, the expedition departed from Saint-Malo harbor on May 23, 1541. Since Roberval was not ready to go at this time, he was to catch up with Cartier as soon as possible. Again, as on the second voyage, the crossing was hampered by poor weather. It was three months before the Canadian coast came into view.

On August 23, 1541, the expedition arrived at Stadacona, where Cartier met with Agona, Donnacona's successor. Cartier told Agona that Donnacona and the other Stadaconans who left with him five years earlier were quite happy to be living in France and had no desire to return. Cartier was lying. He did not reveal that, with the exception of one girl, all the Indians who had gone to France had died there of natural causes. In his meetings with Agona, Cartier sensed that the Stadaconans were no longer as friendly as they had been before.

Cartier's distrust of the Stadaconans increased. Instead of staying near the fort that he and his men had wintered at before, he anchored his ships eight miles west of Stadacona. Situated near the mouth of a river called Rivère du Cap-Rouge, Cartier had his men build a new fort that he named Charlesbourg-Royal. Inside the fort, the French constructed shelter and planted a vegetable garden. In their spare time, the colonists also began looking for precious metals and collecting what they thought were diamonds and gold.

In September, Cartier and a group of his men set off in search of Saguenay. Retracing their earlier route, they passed through the territory of Achelacy, an area that Cartier had briefly visited on the way to Hochelaga. After paying his respects to the chief, Cartier left behind two French youths who were to stay with the Iroquois and learn their language and customs. Traveling on to Hochelaga and Mont Royal, Cartier again encountered the rapids that had blocked his passage in 1535. This time, however, he left his boats behind and followed an Indian portage (carrying boats over land) to reach the navigable part of the river west of the rapids. Cartier's journey brought him to another Indian village, Tutonaguy, where he found four guides who agreed to lead him and his men on to Saguenay.

Once more, circumstances interfered with Cartier's plans. After going a short distance, his guides told him that it would be too difficult to reach Saguenay because another series of dangerous rapids blocked the way. The guides did not tell Cartier that there was another route through the Ottawa River. It remains unclear whether the Indians merely no longer wanted to guide Cartier and his men or whether, for reasons of their own, they had tried to discourage Cartier from going any farther west. What is more certain is that Cartier and his men were forced to turn back. For Cartier, this last effort to locate Saguenay was a failure.

On September 19, 1542 Cartier reached a thriving Iroquoian village located at the foot of a hill, which he christened Mont Réal, or "Mount Royal," and which today is the site of the city of Montreal.

On his way back to the fort, Cartier stopped at the village where he had left the two French boys. To his horror, he found that the boys were gone and the village deserted. Cartier quickly went to Charlesbourg-Royal, where he discovered the fort under threat of attack. Cartier soon learned that in his absence the French had not only treated the Indians with contempt, but were also being blamed for an epidemic that had killed several of the villagers.

After talking things over with his crew and the settlers, Cartier decided it was best to wait out the winter and leave in the spring. During the winter, however, skirmishes with the Indians became a constant fact of life; no fewer than thirty-five Frenchmen died as the result of hostilities. To add to Cartier's frustration, he had still received no word from Roberval announcing his arrival.

By early June 1542, Cartier had enough and ordered the crew and settlers to prepare to return to France. By the end of June, Cartier had reached the harbor of St. John's, Newfoundland. To his surprise, he met Roberval and his four ships there. Roberval ordered Cartier to turn his ships around and sail back to Stadacona. Cartier realized that this would excite mutiny among his crew and the settlers. Instead, he waited until nightfall and then slipped out from the harbor and made for the open sea. By October 1542, almost a year after he had left Saint-Malo, Cartier was safely home. He never again left France.

7

NEW FRANCE: A FORGOTTEN DISCOVERY

By the people of Canada and Hochelaga it was said, That here is the land of Saguenay, which is rich and wealthy in precious stone.
        —Jacques Cartier, *The Voyages of Jacques Cartier*, c. 1565

By mid October 1542, Cartier and his ships had once more safely found their way home, but as it turned out, the "gold" Cartier's men had discovered was pyrite, or fool's gold, and Cartier's "diamonds" were worthless pieces of quartz. Cartier had also failed in his quest to reach Saguenay, but the king was initially more concerned with other matters, especially Cartier's abandonment of Roberval. In the end, Francis I decided not to charge or punish Cartier in any way, and in fact made him a gift of the two ships used in his last expedition. But there would be no more journeys to the New World, at least none sponsored by the crown. Cartier's days as the king's explorer were over.

The mineral pyrite is iron sulfide, a compound of iron and sulfur. Its strong resemblance to gold has tricked many, earning it the name "fool's gold." Cartier was one of those taken in by the rich, brassy, gold-like color of pyrite, which is named from the Greek prefix "pyr" meaning fire. Today the stone is a favorite among rock collectors.

Cartier's failure to find Saguenay had shattered the king's hopes of establishing a prosperous French empire in the New World. Compounding Francis's disappointment was the news that Roberval's settlement had failed to take root in Canada. Like Cartier, Roberval and the other settlers could not withstand the harsh Canadian winters nor establish peaceful relations with the Iroquois Indians. Within a year, Roberval and his ships had returned to France.

Francis now viewed his Canadian lands with disgust. He felt that Canada was little more than a country inhabited by savages, with nothing of value to offer France and a climate that made settlement all but impossible. There was no sense in pursuing further exploration. Not only did the king lose interest in Cartier, but he completely abandoned his efforts to colonize North America. It was nearly fifty years before another French king would send explorers there.

As for the kingdom of Saguenay, it continued to appear on many European maps well into the seventeenth century and then it, too, disappeared forever, except in the form of a river in southern Quebec that bears its name. The fabled kingdom never existed except in the imaginations of the Indians who told the stories that appealed to greedy Frenchmen.

Despite France's neglect of her New World lands, Cartier's voyages did open up the way for further exploration and

Whaling was a growth industry in Cartier's time. Once whales were sighted and the captain gave orders, whaleboats, each manned by six men, would be lowered to give chase. When the boat almost touched the whale's huge back, the officer on board would call to the harpooner at the bow oar to stand, turn, and strike. It was a dangerous job, and the lives of all six men hung on the skill and timing of the two officers in charge.

trade as French fishermen, hunters, whalers, and fur trappers came to Canada to make their fortunes from the abundant natural resources it contained. Cartier's travels also laid the groundwork for how the French would carry out future exploration and settlement in North America. The ways in which Cartier dealt with the many different Indian tribes he encountered—learning their languages, trading, and living among them—were used by other French explorers who came to North America.

89

The Spanish tended to exploit and incite hostilities with and among the Indians that they encountered, while the French never sought to engage in open conflict with the natives. Instead, they were interested in establishing commercial relations with them. Early on, Cartier had realized the value of learning the languages and customs of the tribes he encountered, even to the extent of leaving French youths to live among the Indians and learn their ways.

Viewing Another Culture

Unlike the Spanish, who adopted the term Columbus had introduced, the French never used the term "Indian" to describe the native inhabitants of North America. They usually referred to the tribespeople as *sauvages* (savages), *peaux-rouges* (redskins), or *indigènes* (natives). Despite his careful recording of the customs and culture of the Indians, Cartier never viewed them as the equals of Europeans. By the seventeenth century, when the French again came to the St. Lawrence, they found that the Indians Cartier had encountered upriver had disappeared. The villages, along with the French forts at Stadacona, Hochelaga, and Charlesbourg-Royal, had vanished as if they had never existed.

Europeans established numerous trading stations to exchange goods with the natives they encountered. Glass beads were inexpensive to Europeans and were popular among the Indians, who exchanged furs for them. These bead ornaments are from Fort Mandan, North Dakota.

Despite his eagerness to trade with the Indians, Cartier, like many other Europeans, never regarded them as much more than savages, though he seems at times to have recognized their sophistication. Eventually, this condescension gave rise to hostility between the French and the Indians. In addition, the taking of Indian land, disputes over trade, the French fondness for kidnapping Indians, and other acts of hostility insured that animosity prevailed. This antagonism proved costly to the French; without the goodwill of the Indians, colonization in North America proved even more difficult than it otherwise would have been.

8

THE BOLDEST SPIRIT

On this said Wednesday [1 September 1557] at about five o'clock in the morning died Jacques Cartier.

—Official notice, September 1, 1557,
The Voyages of Jacques Cartier

For the remainder of his life, Jacques Cartier appeared perfectly content to stay close to home. The two vessels that Francis I had given to him in appreciation for his service to France were put to use in the merchant marine. Cartier enjoyed a life of some comfort; besides his ships, he owned a house with a small garden in Saint-Malo and a farm in the nearby village of Limoïlou. According to local records, one of Cartier's favorite pastimes was attending baptisms at the Catholic church. He also had a reputation as a drinker, and could be found with other sailors and adventurers at the local tavern, where he no doubt captivated his audience with tales of his adventures.

This is the title page of the English edition of Cartier's *Shorte and Briefe Narration of the two Navigations and Discoveries to the Northweast partes called Newe France*, published in 1580.

¶ A SHORTE AND
briefe narration of the two
Nauigations and Discoueries
to the Northweast partes called
NEWE FRAVNCE:

First translated out of French into Italian, by that famous
learned man *Gio : Bapt : Ramusius*, and now turned
into English by *Iohn Florio* : Worthy the reading of all Venturers, Trauellers,
and Discouerers.

IMPRINTED AT LON-
don, by H. Bynneman, dvvelling
in Thames streate, neere vnto
Baynardes Castell.

Anno Domini. 1580.

In 1557, Cartier became ill when an epidemic of the plague spread throughout the French country- side. He died on September 1, 1557, at the age of sixty-six. He was survived by his wife, Catherine des Granches, and he left behind an astonishing archive of his three journeys to North America. In time, these notes, logs, journals, maps, charts, and books passed on to his nephews, who had them published. Despite Cartier's contributions to the history of exploration, it was another century before the world truly recognized what he had accomplished.

Today, the importance of Cartier's discoveries is unquestioned. He helped to establish the French presence in Canada, opening the way for future French exploration and settlement. His meticulously detailed notes, diaries, and maps have aided modern historians and geographers, adding to their knowl- edge of sixteenth-century navigational techniques, maritime technology, and the everyday lives of sixteenth-century seafarers. Cartier's journals are also an invaluable source for modern-day readers to understand how the New World was perceived by Cartier and others of his generation.

Yet for all his successes, Cartier also failed in many important ways. His refusal to sail farther westward along the St. Lawrence River—which, contrary to what he thought, would have been relatively easy to do—cost him another chance to win a king's commission. His heavy-handed relations with the St. Lawrence Iroquois, and his abandonment of Roberval took away from his stature as an explorer as well as his reputation as an honorable man.

Still, Cartier was a rarity among European mariners. He could honestly claim that he never lost a single man on any of his sea voyages; what casualties the French suffered under his command came as the result of disease and warfare with the Indians. Cartier was coolheaded and intelligent. Although perfectly capable of making up his own mind and giving orders that his decisions be carried out, Cartier was also known to consult his men on important matters when he felt it necessary to do so.

Cartier's contributions to North American, especially Canadian, history are too numerous to recount. His journals were the first documents ever to record European impressions of Canada. He was painstakingly accurate in his descriptions, making them invaluable for understanding the appearance of the region. They also present a fascinating glimpse of life aboard his ship and reveal Cartier's beliefs about the world, his attitudes toward his journey, and all that he had discovered.

Cartier's accounts of his travels continue to engage modern readers. Many of the place names that he gave to the sites he visited are still in use today. His own name is memorialized throughout Canada on numerous streets, schools, and a bridge.

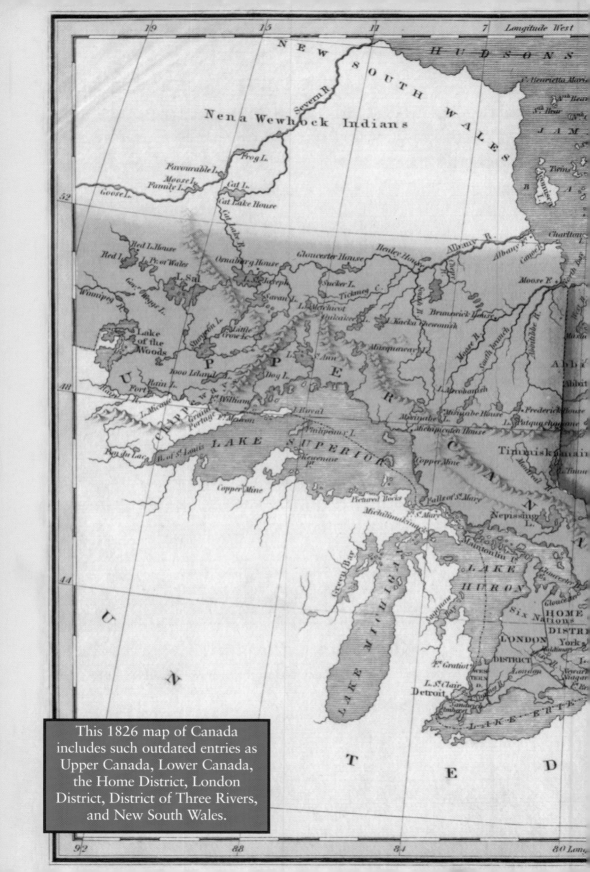

This 1826 map of Canada includes such outdated entries as Upper Canada, Lower Canada, the Home District, London District, District of Three Rivers, and New South Wales.

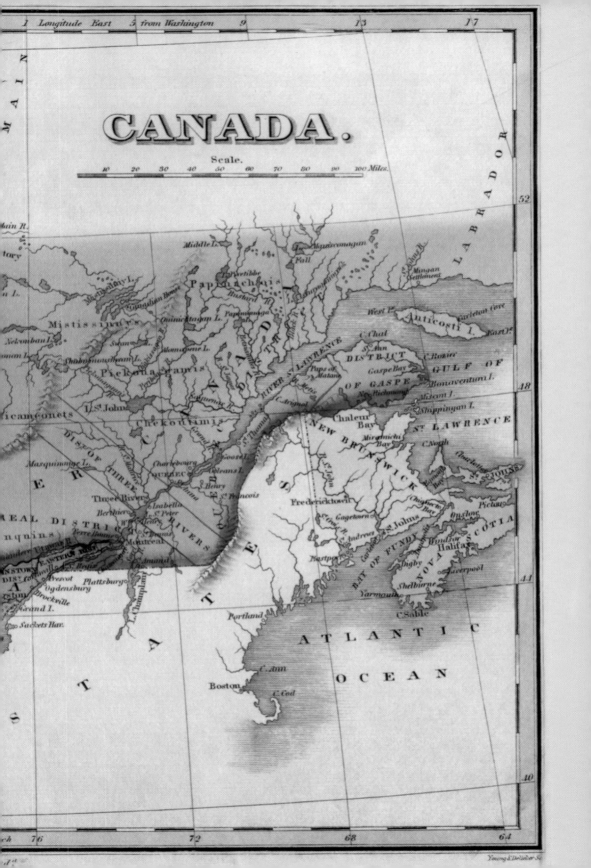

CANADA.

Scale.

10   20   30   40   50   60   70   80   90   100 Miles.

MAINE

LABRADOR

52

Main R.

tory

Middle L.

Maniconagan

Fall

Ouetibbe

Papinachois

Bustard

Papinaguan

Mistissiny's

Nekembau L.

Ouinichtagan L.

Mistassini

Swan L.

Wamagone L.

Shohoshuashuam L.

Picksuckagawis

L. St. Johns

Chekoutimis

West P.

Anticosti I.

Carleton Cove

East P.

Mingan Settlement

C. Chat

St. Ann

DISTRICT

Gaspe Bay

C. Rozier

GULF OF

OF GASPE

Bonaventure I.

New Richmond

Miscou I.

Shippingan I.

18

Icamconets

DIST. OF THREE

Chaleur

Bay

NEW BRUNSWICK

Miramichi

Bay

C. North

ST. LAWRENCE

Charlotte

Bay

ST. JOHNS

Masquinunge L.

Charlesbourg

QUEBEC

R. St. Thomas

Orleans I.

St. Henry

St. Francois

R. St. John

Fredericktown

RIVERS

Three Rivers

Berthier

Isabella

L. St. Peter

Gagetown

St. Andrews

St. Johns

Chaseto

Bay

Onslow

Pictou

NOVA SCOTIA

Halifax

AL DISTRICT

nquins

Montreal

Annand

Portland

Montreal

NSTOWN

EASTERN

Cornwall

St. Regis

Prescot

Ogdensburg

Plattsburg

Brockville

Grand I.

Sackets Har.

Eastport

Windsor

Digby

Liverpool

BAY OF FUNDY

Shelburne

Yarmouth

C. Sable

STATE

Portland

C. Ann

Boston

C. Cod

ATLANTIC

OCEAN

76   72   68   64

Cartier's Legacy

The province of Quebec has never forgotten Cartier. One of the most popular gathering places in Montreal is Place Jacques-Cartier located in Old Montreal, which faces the St. Laurent, or St. Lawrence, River. Here, visitors can enjoy street entertainment, dine at one of the many sidewalk cafés or restaurants, or visit some of Montreal's museums and other important landmarks. The Cartier-Brébeuf National Historic Site, located on the north shore of the Saint Charles River in Quebec, commemorates the period in 1535–1536 when Jacques Cartier and his shipmates wintered near the village of Stadacona in Quebec.

The Jacques-Cartier River, located in south-central Quebec, bounds the Jacques-Cartier Provincial Park, considered one of Canada's most scenic spots. And every year some 43 million automobiles cross the Jacques-Cartier Bridge that spans the St. Lawrence River and Seaway—a massive navigational system of canals, lakes, and rivers that link the St. Lawrence River with the Great Lakes—facing St. Helens's Island.

These metal *stelae*, built in 1977, commemorating the 1534 landing of Cartier at Gaspé Peninsula, stand at the Musee de la Gaspé, Quebec. The ancient Appalachians begin here, stretching over 1,500 miles to Alabama. It is easy to imagine that one has reached the end of the earth when sea mists shroud these sculpted cliffs. The Micmac, who occupied this land when Cartier arrived, thought so because they called it "Gespeg," meaning "the place where the land ends."

Ships bearing his name travel the same waters that he sailed nearly 500 years ago. Perhaps the finest monuments to Jacques Cartier are those that he himself created. Through his journals, we can begin to understand the mind and world of a man who was not afraid to go wherever curiosity and ambition took him and who, in pursuing his dreams, defied conventional thinking. His was among the boldest of spirits in an age of bold and spirited men.

CHRONOLOGY

1491   Jacques Cartier born in Saint-Malo, France.

1532   Cartier accepts King Francis I's offer to undertake a journey to the New World.

1534   Cartier leaves Saint-Malo on April 20 for his first journey to North America. Returns to France on September 5.

1535   Cartier leaves for his second journey to North America. Discovers mouth of the St. Lawrence River.

1535–1536   Cartier and his crew spend the winter at St. Charles River.

1536   Cartier returns home to Saint-Malo on July 16.

1540 Cartier appointed captain general of a third expedition.

1542 Cartier names Mount Royal, the future site of Montreal.

1541 Cartier learns that Jean-François de la Rocque de Roberval will lead the new expedition. Leaves for this third and final voyage to North America on May 23.

1542 Cartier refuses Roberval's orders to return to Canada and instead sails home.

1557 Cartier dies in Saint-Malo on September 1 at the age of sixty-six.

1565 Account of Cartier's first voyage is published in Italian.

GLOSSARY

agile Characterized by quickness, lightness, and ease of movement; nimble.

antagonism An unfriendly feeling.

commission To give someone permission to carry out a duty or an office.

epidemic An outbreak of a contagious disease that spreads rapidly.

flotilla A fleet of ships.

Great Lakes Five connected freshwater lakes located between the borders of the United States and Canada. The lakes are Lake Superior, Lake Huron, Lake Erie, Lake Michigan, and Lake Ontario.

inlet   A bay or cove.

longboat   A large boat with oars that was often found on merchant ships.

mariner   A sailor, or navigator.

Northwest Passage   The sought-after shortcut through the New World to China, which would have provided a more direct trade route between Europe and Asia.

papal decree   An order or law made by the pope.

Papal Bull of 1493   A papal bull issued in 1493 by Pope Alexander VI, which symbolically divided the world down the middle of the Atlantic Ocean. According to the document, the pope granted Spain the rights to all newly discovered lands in the New World, while all the land east of the line, including Africa and India, belonged to Portugal.

peninsula   A land area surrounded on three sides by water.

plague   A contagious, often fatal epidemic disease spread by infected vermin, especially fleas from infected rats.

portage   The act of carrying canoes or other small vessels across land to avoid waters that are dangerous or unnavigable.

privateer   A private ship owner who is authorized by his government, usually during war, to attack enemy vessels.

pyrite   A yellow mineral formed from sulfur and iron and often mistaken for gold; sometimes called fool's gold.

rapids   Swiftly moving waters or waterfalls.

rigging   Ropes on ships used to control and support the masts and sails.

stelae   Upright stone slabs or pillars engraved with an inscription or design and used as a monument or grave marker.

strait   A narrow passageway connecting two bodies of water.

topography   Study of the earth's terrain or landforms.

FOR MORE INFORMATION

Archives National/National Archives
535, Avenue Viger Est
Montreal, Quebec H2L 2P3
(514) 873-6000
Web site: http://www.anq.gouv.qc.ca

Canadian Museum of Civilization
100 Laurier Street
P.O. Box 3100
Station B, Gatineau, Quebec J8X 4H2
(819) 776-7000 or (800) 555-5621
Web site: http://www.civilization.ca/contact/contacte.html

Web Sites

Due to the changing nature of Internet links, the Rosen Publishing Group, Inc., has developed an online list of Web sites related to the subject of this book. This site is updated regularly. Please use this link to access the list:

http://www.rosenlinks.com/lee/jaca/

FOR FURTHER READING

Averill, Esther Holden. *Cartier Sails the St. Lawrence.* New York: Harper & Brothers, 1956.

Blashfield, Jean. *Cartier: Jacques Cartier in Search of the Northwest Passage.* Minneapolis, MN: Compass Point Press, 2001.

Coulter, Tony. *Jacques Cartier, Samuel de Champlain, and the Explorers of Canada.* New York: Chelsea House Publishers, 1993.

Harmon, Daniel E. *Jacques Cartier and the Exploration of Canada.* Philadelphia: Chelsea House Publishers, 2001.

Mason, Antony. *The Children's Atlas of Exploration: Follow in the Footsteps of the Great Explorers.* Brookfield, CT: Millbrook Press, 1993.

Syme, Ronald. *Cartier: Finder of the St. Lawrence.* New York: William Morrow and Company, 1958.

BIBLIOGRAPHY

Bedini, Silvio, ed. *The Christopher Columbus Encyclopedia*. New York: Simon & Schuster, 1992.

Cartier, Jacques. *Navigations to Newe Fraunce.* Translated by John Florio. Ann Arbor, MI: University Microfilms, Inc., 1966.

Cartier, Jacques. The Voyages of Jacques Cartier. Toronto: University of Toronto Press, 1993.

Eccles, W. J. *France in America*. New York: Harper & Row, 1972.

Elliott, J. H. *The Old World and the New, 1492–1650*. New York: Cambridge University Press, 1992.

Kagan, Richard L., and Geoffry Parker. *Spain, Europe, and the Atlantic: Essays in Honor of John H. Elliott*. New York: Cambridge University Press, 1995.

Meinig, D. W. *The Shaping of America: A Geographical Perspective on 500 Years of History, Volume 1, Atlantic America 1492–1800*. New Haven, CT: Yale University Press, 1986.

Morison, Samuel Eliot. *The European Discovery of America. Vol. 1: The Northern Voyages, A.D. 500–1600*. New York: Oxford University Press, 1993.

Parkman, Francis. *France and England in North America, Volume 1*. New York: The Library of America, 1983.

Parkman, Francis. *The Canadian Frontier, 1534–1760*. Albequerque, NM: University of New Mexico, 1974.

Quinn, David B., and Richard Hakluyt, eds. *A Study Introductory to the facsimile edition of Richard Hakluyt's DIVERS VOYAGES (1582) to which is added A SHORTE AND BRIEFE NARRATION OF THE TWO NAVIGATIONS TO NEWE FRANCE, Volumes 1 and 2*. New York: Barnes and Noble Inc., 1967.

Toye, William. *Cartier Discovers the St. Lawrence*. New York: Oxford University Press, 1971.

INDEX

About the Author

Meg Greene earned a bachelor's degree in history at Lindenwood College in St. Charles, Missouri, and master's degrees from the University of Nebraska at Omaha and the University of Vermont. Ms. Greene is the author of twelve other books, writes regularly for *Cobblestone* magazine and other publications, and serves as a contributing editor for Suite101.com's "History for Children." She lives in Virginia.

Photo Credits

Series Design and Layout

Tahara Hasan

Editor

Annie Sommers